The Fragile Elegance

With each drip drop, a battle fought,
The snowman sighs, his head is caught.
Looking quite round, now rather thin,
Dieting hard before the spin.

Sleds go sliding down one last hill,
Kids giggle loud, they just can't chill.
Every snowball, a fleeting jest,
Winter's end is such a test.

Crystalline Memories in the Warming Sun

The sun's warm rays, a sly sneak peek,
Melting dreams of frosty chic.
Icicles dangle, all on a whim,
They tumble like champs, a frozen hymn.

Hot chocolate cups go cold and sad,
The marshmallows float, it's just plain mad!
Sipping slowly, the laughter brews,
As tales of snowball fights amuse.

Original title:
Ephemeral Ice

Copyright © 2024 Creative Arts Management OÜ
All rights reserved.

Author: George Mercer
ISBN HARDBACK: 978-9916-94-478-3
ISBN PAPERBACK: 978-9916-94-479-0

Surrender to the Snow

Fluffy flakes swirl, like a dance,
Snowmen wobble, give winter a chance.
With carrot noses and button eyes,
They plot their mischief, oh what a surprise!

Sleds zoom past, oh what a thrill,
Chasing snowballs, it's a great skill.
But who will slip on that icy patch?
Laughter erupts with every bad catch!

Frosty cheeks and rosy red noses,
Hot cocoa beckons, as winter dozes.
Sneaky squirrels, in fluffy attire,
Taunt us with antics that never expire!

As the sun peeks in, the magic will fade,
Yet giggles remain in this snowy parade.
So let's not fret, let's leap and glide,
For winter's charm is a cheerful ride!

Glacial Artistry in the Twilight Hour

Puddle paintings on the ground,
Colors mix, oh what a sound!
Slippery steps make folks go slip,
Chasing their balance, a comic trip.

Frosty mittens, now out of style,
Finding the sun brings a goofy smile.
No more snowflakes on the nose,
Just muddy boots and soggy toes.

Whispering Winds of a Thawing Night

The winds start whispering tales anew,
Of hot cocoa parties and baked foo.
Furry hats dance on doggies' heads,
As snowflakes first join the rubber sleds.

Under the stars, the warm air hums,
As winter bows and springtime drums.
Croaking frogs now join in the jest,
Nature's laughter is truly the best.

The Last Flicker of Winter

Old snowmen melt with a frown,
As kids chase puddles in town.
Sleds park sad by the lawn,
While hot cocoa dreams have gone!

Icicles hang like candy canes,
Merry-go-rounds freeze their trains.
The winter's last jolly prank,
Is turning our boots into sank!

A Formless Frost

Jack Frost dances, what a sight!
With frosty breath at morning light.
He plays tag with a runaway mitt,
While snowflakes giggle, oh so lit!

A snowball fights without a goal,
But everyone ends up in a hole.
Chasing chill, we slip and slide,
Like penguins on a slippery ride!

Shadows in Ice

Shadows stretch, they flip and flop,
On a frozen pond, we take a hop.
But oh dear! A wobbly shoe,
Turns ice capades to a zoo!

Thin ice whispers, 'Take a chance!'
As we swirl in a clumsy dance.
Cackles echo, laughter rings,
Winter's folly, oh what fun it brings!

Moments of Glacial Grace

They call it grace, but I disagree,
Tripped on a snowflake, oh woe is me!
A graceful glide turned into a bell,
As I crash like a glacier, oh well!

We tumble, we roll, we're full of glee,
Chasing snowflakes like wild bumblebees.
The frosty air is filled with cheer,
As winter's chuckles draw us near!

Fleeting Crystals on a Winter's Breath

Snowflakes fall, a dance so spry,
They snowball fight, oh me, oh my!
Catch them quick, they vanish fast,
Laughing as their moments pass.

Icicles hang, like teeth so long,
They drip and drop a silly song.
Watch your head, the plop is near,
Nature's joke, bring on the cheer!

Transient Patterns of Frosted Whispers

Patterns form then fade away,
Like my plans for the big buffet!
Caught in a moment, they shimmer bright,
Then giggle soft, vanished from sight.

Doodles drawn on chilly panes,
Caffeine spills, oh what a stain!
Smudged and smeared, a frosty joke,
With every sip, more laughs evoke!

The Last Dance of Winter's Veil

Dancing shadows on the ground,
Sipping cocoa, the laughter's found.
Pretend to slip, but what a show,
Oh look, it's the winter tango!

Last twirls on the frozen lake,
Snowmen wobble, what's at stake?
They tip and topple, hats askew,
A frosty party, just for you!

Shards of Time in a Melting World

Moments drip like melting ice,
Flavor bursts, oh, that's so nice!
Lick a cone, then it's a race,
Chasing drips all over the place!

Time slips like a slippery fish,
A frosty wish, oh, what a dish!
In this world, giggles resound,
As we chase joy, round and round!

Fleeting Reflections in the Icy Stillness

Once I slipped on a frozen pond,
My dignity flew like a wandering swan.
I waved at friends who just couldn't aid,
As I made my grand entrance, a clumsy cascade.

A raccoon watched, grimacing with glee,
I might be the punchline of creature comedy.
Yet I laughed as I flailed, a sight to behold,
In this fragile dance, my laughter turned bold.

The Briefest of Silences on a Crystal Sheet

On a winter's morn, I sought a glide,
But the ice had secrets it chose to hide.
A step, a slip, oh what a sight,
As I rocketed forward like a blimp in flight.

The silence broke with my hiccuped fall,
The snowflakes tittered, the trees stood tall.
I told them jokes, but they didn't reply,
Just glittering laughter, under the blue sky.

An Instant of Cold Beneath the Radiant Sun

I built a snowman with charisma and flair,
But the sun had plans to melt away my heir.
With a wink and a nod, he began to flop,
Giving me a masterpiece that was ready to drop.

I shouted, "Don't go! You were my best mate!"
But he splashed into puddles; it was too late.
I waved goodbye to his carrot-nosed grin,
Thinking, what fun, until spring rolled in.

The Icy Mirage of a Warming World

In a land where snowflakes now blink and fade,
I found a snowball that someone had made.
I threw it with force, but it didn't adhere,
Just vaporized softly, as if it could hear.

The kids laughed and pointed, their faces aglow,
As I pranced around in an ill-fated show.
We declared it a game, a sport of the light,
Chasing the drip-drop; what a silly sight!

Shivering Surrender

In the fridge, I found my fate,
A frozen treat that's gone too late.
A popsicle with a lofty dream,
Now just a puddle, or so it seems.

I wore my scarf, just like a king,
But lost my grip on that slippery thing.
I slipped and slid, I danced with glee,
A frosty ballet for all to see.

Frosted Echoes

In the morning light, a crunch underfoot,
I think it's crunchy snow, but it's my boot!
With every step, I hear a snap,
What a glorious, noisy winter trap!

The trees are dressed in glittery gear,
But it's just a fashion faux pas, I fear.
They wobble and shiver, they seem to giggle,
As branches shimmy, oh, how they wiggle!

Drifting Snow

Oh look, a flake! It's like a feather,
I catch it, but it's gone—so clever!
Playing tag with the biting breeze,
Chasing whimsies that don't appease.

The snowman grins with a carrot nose,
But later he frowns as the sunlight shows.
His smile drips down to a puddled fate,
Oh Mr. Snow, you've lost your state!

The Wintry Mirage

I saw a snow fort, oh what a sight,
But it was just a pile of powdery light.
I imagined battles, fought with snowballs,
Instead, I flopped – triggered a slew of falls.

The laughter echoed, birds took flight,
As I looked up, what a silly sight!
Flakes fell down like confetti bright,
A winter party, oh what a delight!

Vanishing Patterns

A snowman made of hopes and dreams,
Melting on the grass, or so it seems.
He's wearing buttons made of gum,
But now he's just a puddly thumb.

The icicles hang like frozen spears,
Tickling noses, bringing cheers.
Yet one by one, they slip and slide,
As laughter echoes, they start to hide.

Frosty footprints lead nowhere fast,
Chasing the chill, how long can it last?
A comedy of slides and falls,
Ice jokes framed on frosty walls.

The sun arrives, the party's done,
Whispers of warmth, oh what fun!
And in the end, through all the fray,
We laugh at winter's quick ballet.

Silent Fragments

Once a frozen lake, so grand and vast,
Now just a sheet of memories past.
Skaters twirling with effortless grace,
Fall on their backs, it's quite the place!

Snowflakes dance like tiny sprites,
Whispering secrets of chilly nights.
But in a blink, they vanish away,
Leaving us laughing at their display.

The chilly breeze plays peek-a-boo,
With winter's chill, it tickles you.
Snowballs thrown, then all is quiet,
Silence shatters; a snowball riot!

A winter's tale in fleeting time,
Each laugh and slip, oh what a rhyme!
Underneath the moonlight's trance,
We giggle as we take our chance.

Chasing the Frost

Frosty noses and frozen toes,
Chasing sunshine wherever it goes.
A snowball war erupts with delight,
Giggles and squeals in frosty flight.

Pine trees adorned with glistening ice,
Nature's jewels, oh so nice!
But with a giggle, they start to weep,
Falling down in a snowy heap.

The playful breeze gives a mischievous nudge,
Plotting with snowflakes to make us judge.
Who can catch them before they melt?
Tickling our toes, the laughter is felt.

Racing the sun in a shimmering show,
Each glistening patch begins to glow.
We twirl and spin until we're beat,
In the game of winter, oh what a treat!

Glacial Euphoria

In a land where cold confetti flies,
Tiny icicles dance, oh what a surprise!
Snowflakes tickle like tiny fingers,
While laughter and snowball chaos lingers.

A trip on ice, it's quite the thrill,
Who needs a fall when you can spill?
Giggles erupt as faces plant,
In the quest for fun, you know we can't!

Chasing snowmen made really weird,
With carrot noses that sometimes disappeared.
They grin big until they drip,
Ah, winter's fun on a playful trip!

But as the sun brings warmth and cheer,
The icy joy just won't adhere.
We laugh as we see it fade away,
And plan for icy games another day!

The Frostbite of Time

In winter's grasp, my nose turns red,
I trip on snow, wish I'd stayed in bed.
My breath creates clouds, a visible show,
Yet I fumble and tumble on ice like a pro.

The snowmen wear scarves, looking quite grand,
While I slip and slide, can't take a stand.
They mock me in silence, those frosty folks,
As I cringe at my fate, tripping on jokes.

A snowball in hand, I aim for the throne,
But it lands on my head, I'm feeling alone.
With laughter echoing from every tree,
I've become the punchline of winter's spree.

So here I embrace every slip, every fall,
The laughter of winter, the best of it all.
For every good tumble just warms up my heart,
In this chilly, funny, frostbitten art.

Illusive Winter

Snowflakes dance lightly, like petals in flight,
They tease and they twirl, what a glorious sight!
While I'm busy wiping my glasses anew,
They land on my nose, the jokers in blue.

In a flurry of white, I think I might soar,
But I'm met with soft ground that says, 'Not anymore!'
With arms spread wide, I fly through the air,
A graceful swan, if swans did despair.

Winter's a prankster with slippery floors,
She laughs as I tumble and roll through the doors.
The hot cocoa's waiting, a warm little cheer,
But first, let me battle this snow without fear.

So I race to my mug, with froth like a crown,
Then spill it all over, oh, what a clown!
With a chuckle, I sip on my frothy delight,
In this frosty charade, I'm the star of the night.

Dappled Glaze

The sun peeks out with a playful grin,
Melting the ice, oh where to begin?
With puddles forming, reflections they seize,
I slide like a penguin, where's my expertise?

Laughter erupts from the melting snow,
While I pirouette, I can't seem to flow.
A dab of moisture adds sparkle on ground,
I discover the joy in this slip 'n' astound.

Every shimmer's a tease, a light-hearted game,
As I leap and I spin, I feel no shame.
But just as I bask in the wintertime tease,
I'm met with a splash, saying, "Oh, not with ease!"

So I gather my courage, my laughter, my pride,
In this dappled environment, I'll glide and slide.
With smiles in the rain, I bid winter farewell,
In this silly caper, I've found my own spell.

Tides of Frost's Farewell

The frost starts to melt, it drips and it plops,
As I hurry along, my enthusiasm hops.
The world turns to slush, oh what a delight,
I'm swimming through puddles, it feels just right.

I wiggle and dance, in this mushy terrain,
Every step is a giggle, a comical gain.
With icebergs now shrinking, my heart begins to sing,
This wintery chaos, the joy that it brings!

But the temperatures rise with each playful leap,
And soon I will miss the cold's icy sweep.
Though snowflakes may scatter, their laughter remains,
In giggles of puddles, I shuffle the lanes.

So here's to all frosty and whimsical dreams,
As I elegantly waddle, I burst at the seams.
For winter may recede and the chill may subside,
But the laughter of ice lives on with a slide!

The Crystal's Lament

In a world of frosty sighs,
Where icicles wear winter ties,
A snowman trips, he took a chance,
His carrot nose? A slippery dance!

The flakes come down, a chaotic sight,
With each gust, a brilliant flight,
But snowballs fly, not always fair,
With snowmen crying, 'Life's a cold affair!'

Through chilly days and icy nights,
Mittens lost in snowball fights,
The frosty winds with giggles tease,
While penguins waddle with utmost ease!

So cherish laughter, though it's brief,
In this ice world, oh what a relief!
For even crystals shed a tear,
As sunny days draw ever near!

Elysium of Cold

In a land where shivers reign,
Snowflakes dance like silly trains,
A polar bear dons shades so bright,
Waving at fish in frosty flight!

Frosty treats and snowball glee,
Frostbite? Nah! That's just a spree,
Kids on sleds scream with delight,
As snowmen guard the frosty night.

A penguin slips, lands on its rear,
With frosty giggles, brings us cheer,
In this realm of snow and ice,
We trade our warmth for chilly spice!

So raise a toast with ice-cold beer,
To winter's charm and frosty cheer,
As laughter echoes through the freeze,
In this frosty land, we find our ease!

Frozen Reflections

There once was a pond, shiny and slick,
Where ducks played tag, a bold little trick,
A figure skater took a big leap,
But ended up in a pile, oh deep!

The ice was thick, or so they thought,
But soon they found, it really caught,
A squirrel on skates, quite the mighty show,
Who pirouetted, then fell, oh no!

With every slip, the laughter grew,
As friends yelled, 'Now it's your turn too!'
Snowball fights erupt to ease the pain,
While frosty giggles fill the plain.

And as the sun began to shine,
Melting the fun, oh divine!
Each puddle left a memory sweet,
Of icy antics and frosty feet!

Melodic Chill

In the winter breeze, we hum a tune,
While snowflakes boogie beneath the moon,
A choir of icicles sings with glee,
With a rhythm found in frosty spree.

The bunnies hop in winter's light,
Wearing tiny boots, a comical sight,
While they leap and bound across the snow,
Giving ice a run for its frosty glow!

Twirling frost in a jolly spin,
Where frozen hearts can't help but grin,
As skaters glide with cheery shouts,
While snowmen dance, full of doubts!

So let's embrace this chilly jest,
With laughter, snowballs, and winter zest,
For in this world of crystal skies,
A merry heart will surely rise!

Transient Solitude

In a frosty park, I tossed a snowball,
It hit a tree and then started to fall.
The squirrel paused, then gave me a stare,
I laughed so hard, it fluffed up its hair.

With winter gear, I looked quite a sight,
A bulky jacket, I could barely write.
The snowflakes danced around my nose,
And landed right on my frozen toes.

My laughter echoed in the chilly air,
While neighbors yelled, "There's ice in your hair!"
I looked like a snowman, full of glee,
Yet stumbled and fell—just me and the tree!

Now spring is near, the ice starts to gleam,
But winter's blunders are my favorite theme.
I'll keep my cap and my lighthearted grin,
Till I'm again caught in the winter's spin.

Fragments of a Shimmering Chill

A penguin waddles in my backyard,
He slips and slides, it's really quite hard.
His flippers flail like a low-budget show,
With each little tumble, I burst out in woe.

Icicles hang like teeth from the eaves,
Just watch your head or it's ice that deceives.
With one little slip, I'm embracing the ground,
Joyful laughter is all that surrounds.

Frozen doughnuts on branches look sweet,
I laugh and munch, winter's little treat.
Each bite is chilly, my teeth start to chatter,
But giggles escape; what does it matter?

As mornings thaw, I'll miss the cold hug,
But that crazy penguin, he'll keep me snug.
With memories of laughter, I bid winter goodbye,
Till next year's antics will catch my eye!

The Last Breath of Winter

A snowman named Fred had a garden of dreams,
With carrot nose flopped and a hat full of beams.
He stood all day with his frosty grin,
But looked quite worried as the thaw began.

His best friend, a snowflake, said, "Don't be blue,"
"We'll slide down the hill just for a view!"
They tumbled and giggled on frosty white rides,
Until they both sprawled, giggling wide-eyed.

The sun came out, now things got so grim,
Fred started to melt, his chances quite slim.
"Hold on tight, my friend, we'll have some fun!"
But Fred lost a limb, "Well… that's just my pun."

With puddles forming where laughter could thrive,
Fred waved goodbye like a last winter jive.
I'll create new jokes as spring flowers bloom,
But today I'll remember, let's shrug off the gloom!

Echoes of an Icy Veil

Under a blanket of sparkling frost,
We built a fortress, then giggled and tossed.
My friend took aim with a snowy sphere,
Hit me right in the face—oh dear me, oh dear!

Later, I found my scarf draped on a tree,
It looked like a flag, waving just for me.
I shout to the wind, "Bring it back, my friend!"
But all I got back were giggles that blend.

As snowflakes fell from a cloudy gray dome,
I danced through the flakes like I was at home.
The cold kissed my cheeks and invited a game,
But tripping on ice, I was the one to blame!

So here's to the days of slipping and sliding,
To laughter and warmth where the joy is abiding.
When winter retreats, with its chill and delight,
I'll dream of my antics in the moonlight.

Ethereal Fragments of a Frozen Dream

A snowman tried to take a ride,
But his carrot nose began to slide.
He waddled on the frozen ground,
And fell on his face—oh what a sound!

The penguins danced, all in a twist,
Slipping and sliding, they couldn't resist.
Their bow ties slipped, making them frown,
While a snowflake stuck to a big fat clown.

Frosty scarves were all the rage,
But melted quickly on every stage.
A snowball fight turned into a slip,
With everyone down, just taking a dip!

When winter leaves with a comical jolt,
All that's left is a soggy vault.
So here's our toast to flurries brief,
Next season's laugh, our winter's chief!

Vanishing Echoes on a Glacial Surface

Upon the lake, a grand old moose,
Played ice hockey with a goose.
But with a swing, that stick did break,
They both just flopped—oh what a quake!

A beard of icicles, looking nice,
Broke off and tumbled—oh, what a slice!
The fisherman laughed till he nearly cried,
As his hat sailed away with the giddy tide.

Tiny seals wore snowflakes like hats,
As they chased their tails, rolling like bats.
But the sun peeked out, and heard their plight,
And giggled warm rays, melting their night.

A penguin in shades, oh what a scene,
Waving goodbye to frosty cuisine.
With winter's humor fading fast,
They'll soon find a sun, making ice their past!

Temporary Glimmers of Chilling Beauty

The frost on my windows glimmered bright,
But missed the chance to take a flight.
It slid down smooth, with a sputtering sound,
Leaving behind a frosty mound.

Ski bunnies learned to slide and spin,
Until they tripped, and snorted in.
With snowballs flying, joy was the aim,
Until someone yelled, "Hey! Who is to blame?"

Ice cream cones come from nippy nights,
But dripped much quicker than we'd claimed rights.
By the time we laughed and took a lick,
The flavors ran, oh, what a trick!

As winter fades and springtime's near,
We'll swap our snowflakes for laughter cheer.
So raise a cup to chilly fun,
Before we bid adieu to the icy run!

A Momentary Chill in the Warmth of Life

A penguin found a hat in the snow,
Thought he looked dapper, thought he'd steal the show.
But with one big bow, the wind gave a blow,
And off went the hat—oh, what a low!

The seal sat tight, with an ice-cream cone,
But each time he took a lick, he felt so alone.
For every delightful flavor he tried,
Melted on down, and he'd just sighed.

The playful gusts gave the kids such glee,
As they built a castle by the old elm tree.
But one swift push made the whole thing fall,
With squeals and laughter, oh, what a brawl!

So cherish the laughs in the frosty glow,
For moments like these, they come and they go.
As warmth ventures forth on this chilly spree,
Let's savor the fun, just you and me!

A Tincture of Snow

The flakes fall down with quite a flair,
As snowmen wobble, gasping for air.
They wear a hat that's far too tight,
And dance around 'til they fall at night.

Snowballs fly like fuzzy grenades,
Bouncing off cheeks and in parades.
Sleds go zooming, oh what a thrill,
Till someone crashes and rolls down the hill.

Frosty friends with carrot noses,
Chasing sunbeams like gentle roses.
They freeze their smiles and laugh so loud,
As winter's mischief attracts a crowd.

But soon they melt with the warming glow,
Leaving behind a puddly show.
"Catch me if you can!" they say with glee,
As drips and drops set their spirits free.

The Ice Heartbeat

With icy hearts that beat with cheer,
We skate around without a fear.
Gliding fast with arms out wide,
Falling often, it's quite a ride!

Wobbling ducks on frozen lakes,
Flap their wings and slip on stakes.
"Just a quick dance," they seem to claim,
But soon they join the slippery game.

A snowball fight turns wild and sweet,
With laughter echoing, oh what a treat!
Frosty giants loom so tall,
But take a tumble, and down they fall!

Cold winds howl with giggling might,
As we embrace the snowy night.
So let's dance with icy fun,
Until the morning chases the sun!

Time's Icy Canvas

The morning light sparkles bright,
On a canvas of frozen delight.
Brushes made of snowflakes dip,
Creating art with every slip!

Funny faces with coal black eyes,
Proudly placed under grayish skies.
A masterpiece of frozen grace,
Until the sun comes, quickening pace.

Every flick and twist is grand,
Yet melts away like a fleeting brand.
With giggles echoing through the chill,
We paint our dreams with laughter still.

As puddles form in the waking sun,
We giggle at all the silly fun.
Time laughs as it twirls away,
Leaving traces for another day.

Ethereal Gleam

On a twinkling night, snowflakes gleam,
Starlit whispers turn to a dream.
Fairies skate on the lotus pond,
Twirling round with a friendly bond.

Inside the snowman, snowballs hide,
"Catch me quick!" they playfully bide.
With rolling giggles, they pop right out,
And in the chaos, there's a shout!

Tiny feet leave prints that tease,
In the frosty breath of winter's breeze.
They leap and bound with sprightly grace,
Chasing shadows in a whimsical race.

But dawn will come with warmth so sneaky,
And all the laughter fades, quite cheeky.
For frosty fun can't last the night,
Yet memories twinkle, oh, what a sight!

Fleeting Glistens

Once I saw a snowflake dance,
It twirled around, as if in trance.
But with a shout, it lost its spark,
Down it plopped—oh what a lark!

Out popped a rabbit, quite surprised,
With frosty whiskers, big wide eyes.
It said, "Dear snow, don't be so rash,
I just styled up for a splash!"

So off they went, the hare and flake,
Creating giggles, no mistake.
But soon the sun turned up the heat,
And left them both in a big defeat!

Just as they laughed, they did dissolve,
Life's icy puzzles—none to solve!
And in their wake, a tale was spun,
Of frosty fun, now said and done.

Icebound Wishes

A snowman wished to be a star,
But dreaming large can go too far!
He melted down, oh what a sight,
He turned into a puddle bright!

A fish swam by, with quite a smirk,
"You had ambitions—what a quirk!"
The snowman said, with cheeky glee,
"You just wait, you'll see the real me!"

So as he dripped and draped away,
The fish made plans for winter play.
Together now, both quite a pair,
But next spring came, and left them bare!

Yet in their hearts, the memory glows,
Of wishing big, back when it snowed.
So if you find you wish too much,
Remember fun is just a touch!

The Fragile Throne of Frost

A king made of ice upon his throne,
Thought he ruled over all alone.
But with a sneeze, he cracked in two,
And yelled, "Oh dear, what shall I do?"

His crown rolled off, into a lake,
And fish laughed loud at his mistake!
"You can't freeze here forever, mate,
Get up, warm up, before it's late!"

But the king scoffed, with royal flair,
"I'll rule like this—I do not care!"
Yet seconds later, drips and drops,
He vanished quick—just like his props!

So now they say, the throne is bare,
With fish and frogs rejoicing there.
If you see a crown on the pond's edge,
Laugh for the king—he made a pledge!

Snow-kissed Memories

There once was a snowball, round and bright,
It rolled along, feeling just right.
But with a tumble, down it fell,
And turned to slush—oh what a smell!

A squirrel nearby, with acorn stash,
Thought it was a food-related splash.
He took a bite, and ran away,
Squeaking loudly, "That's not okay!"

Next came a puppy, fresh and spry,
Was eager for fun, as it passed by.
A leap, a slip—a frosty slide,
And off it went, like a roller ride!

So here's to the frosty, fleeting cheer,
The laughter shared, so bright and clear.
Though snow might melt and memories fade,
The joy remains, not a charade!

Moments Lost in a Melting Embrace

A snowman wobbles, oh what a sight,
His carrot nose is losing the fight.
With each warm ray, he starts to drip,
"Please don't let me go!" he gives a quip.

Sleds down the hill, a race to the top,
But who needs speed when you might just plop?
A flurry of giggles fills up the air,
As snow pants squish with a soggy stare.

A cup of hot cocoa, it slips from my hand,
And marvelously spills like a bright, gooey sand.
But who needs the warmth when the cold is so fun?
I'll just dance with puddles, the day's not yet done!

In spring's sneaky touch, all frozen things fade,
But the laughter we share will never cascade.
As ice cream melts, let's feast on the jest,
Moments are sweet, so let's laugh with the rest!

Temporal Designs upon the Snowbound Ground

A snowflake lands, but oh, how it sways,
Its beauty is fleeting, just here for a phase.
It giggles and twirls, whispers, "Catch me quick!"
But lands in a puddle, oh what a trick!

Tiny snow angels wear smiles so bright,
But soon they are gone, like a blink in the night.
With wings made of ice, they wave us goodbye,
'Til spring brings her warmth, and they all wish to fly.

A snowball whizzes and hits me in glee,
But I'll launch one back, just wait and see!
With laughter like thunder, we battle with cheer,
While the frosty world melts all our woes here.

Each icy moment melts down in a blink,
Yet memories linger; oh, let us not sink!
We dance in the dusk as the daylight concedes,
Past winter's designs grow the sweetest of seeds.

The Fragile Light of a Winter's Kiss

A glimmering frost dances on my nose,
Like whispers of winter in delicate prose.
"Catch me if you can!" it twinkles with glee,
But then it all fades, like dreams in your tea.

The icicles hang like jewels from the eaves,
Reminding us all of the flurries and leaves.
Just one tiny poke – oh, what a mistake,
A shower of droplets, for laughter's own sake!

The cold wraps us up in a frigid embrace,
Our breath clouds the air; we're in a race!
As mittens get soggy and noses turn red,
We giggle and tumble, it's pure joy instead.

But when the sun shines, it breaks the best jokes,
As snowflakes retire, giving rise to folks.
We'll cherish the frosts, though they may come and go,
In the fragile light, love will always glow!

Echoes of Chilly Laughter in Twilight

Twilight descends with a shimmering gleam,
The world painted in white, as if from a dream.
We slip on the ice, then we tumble and spin,
But oh, in the laughter, that's where we win!

We build up a fort, a fortress of fluff,
But snowball attacks make it rather tough.
"Take cover!" I yell, but the giggles abound,
With snowflakes like confetti, the joy turns around!

Penguins on ice, waddle by with a grin,
They mock all our tumbles, yet join in the din.
Each slip and each slide, a comedic ballet,
With echoes of laughter that linger and play.

So here's to the moments, both silly and bright,
As frosty delights dance away in the night.
Let's cherish the chill, in this laughter's embrace,
For life's but a journey, wrapped in winter's grace!

Crystalized Moments

In a winter wonderland, I slip and slide,
My lunchbox tumbling, oh, what a ride!
Puddles of laughter form on the ground,
As I chase frozen dreams all around.

Snowflakes giggle as they fall from the sky,
Tickling my cheeks, oh me, oh my!
But I can't catch them, they dance and they prance,
With every quick movement, they laugh in advance.

A snowman grins with a carrot nose,
Wearing my hat, striking a pose.
He'll steal my scarf, he'll take my chair,
What a thief, he doesn't care!

Just when we think the chill will stay,
Sunshine beams, melting the fray.
Moments slip by, but who can complain?
I'll find the ice again, next winter's gain!

Temporary Glaciers

There once was a glacier, big as a house,
A home for a mouse, and perhaps a spouse.
But they packed up their bags, said it's too cold,
Off to the toaster, where the heat unfolds.

The sun came to play, with a smile so bright,
Chasing down icicles, what a funny sight!
The glacier was shrinking, waving its arms,
"Hey, don't leave me! I have my charms!"

With each passing moment, it melted away,
Naked like a toddler, come join the fray!
It slipped on a puddle, let out a loud yelp,
"Just hang on, I swear, I'll learn how to help!"

But as it got thinner, we laughed and we spun,
A grand finale, oh, wasn't it fun?
What was once solid, now puddles of cheer,
Melting away, but I'll see you next year!

Snow's Last Embrace

A last hug from winter, soft and white,
Snowmen in snowsuits, what a sight!
They wave goodbye, as sunlight creeps,
In the game of warmth, everybody sleeps.

Clouds puff out their cheeks, all fluffy and round,
Complaining of warmth, making silly sounds.
"Hey, where's our chill? We had a ball!
Zooming in snowflakes, now nothing at all!"

Noses turning pink, with a funny little dance,
Snowballs are left for a summer romance.
"You won't forget us!" the snowflakes assert,
As they tumble away, in the warm, warm dirt.

So, gather your mittens and stash them away,
The snow will be back for a grand soiree.
Hold your breath for winter, it's quite the tease,
Until then, enjoy the warm summer breeze!

Fleeting Chill

A breath of cold air, it comes and it goes,
I chase after it, but where does it pose?
Ghosts of frost nibble on my toes,
Like sweet candy canes, oh how it flows!

I put on a sweater, a hat and some gloves,
But the chill dances out like a flock of doves.
"Catch me if you can!" it giggles and swirls,
As I tumble and trip through wintery whirls.

Footprints ahead, they vanish like dreams,
With each fleeting moment, it giggles and beams.
Snowflakes wink from the curtain of night,
As I chase the chill, what a peculiar sight!

So raise up your mugs, to the laughter in air,
For wintertime's jesters, without a care!
Though frost may be fleeting, let joy fill the space,
Until we meet again, in a cold embrace!

Shards of Transience

A snowman named Bob told a joke,
But he melted away with a little poke.
His carrot nose wiggled with glee,
"I was just here for the comedy!"

The icicles hung from the roof like a frown,
'Till the sun laughed hard and sent them down.
They splashed in puddles, the water was warm,
"Who knew we were made for such a charm?"

Silly little crystals wore hats made of frost,
Yet they giggled as they realized they were lost.
In a grand parade, they slipped and they slid,
Not quite sure how they ended up hid!

A snowflake once claimed it could make it last,
But waved goodbye, melted down so fast.
"I'll return next winter, just you wait,
With a punchline that'll be first-rate!"

Melting Dreams

In the freezer, a dream once froze,
Woke up one morning with a runny nose.
It grumbled and tumbled like jellybeans,
"Where's my cool? I'm not what I seems!"

The puddle claimed riches, the treasure of buds,
As ants marched by, playing in mud.
"We're wealthy!" they cheered, with laughter and cheer,
But the sun popped through and made it all clear.

A snowflake told tales of heights and despair,
But slipped on its tongue—what a sticky affair!
It fluttered and flapped, tried to be sleek,
"Next time I'll just stick to my peak!"

The winter's a joker, with tricks at its sleeves,
Melting moments like candy that deceives.
So grab your warm socks, pull them up tight,
For laughter is fleeting, let's giggle tonight!

Glimmers of Winter

Glimmers of joy in a frosty night,
Danced with delight, oh what a sight!
Snowflakes performed like stars in a show,
Until they flopped, now just white gooey snow.

The winter winds whispered tales all around,
But the squirrels laughed loud, they really were bound.
"Chilly!" they squeaked, doing flips just in time,
While the frosty air chimed a jingle and rhyme.

A pint-sized snowman wore a top hat so grand,
But tripped on a patch of icy, wet sand.
"Oh dear!" he exclaimed, falling down with a splash,
"What a way for a snow gent to finish his stash!"

Slippery slides turned giggles into roars,
As the ducks waddled by, covered in frosty decor.
With a quack and a squawk, they slipped with pure grace,

Winter's just here for the laugh on our face!

The Dance of Frostflowers

Frostflowers twirled in a beautiful mess,
Spinning and flailing, oh what a dress!
They laughed and they giggled, oh what a sight,
Until the sun peeked, and they took flight.

One frostbud declared, "Let's hold a parade!"
But then came the warmth, and their plans all just swayed.

"Alas! We are tiny!" they shouted with zest,
But their giggles melted, it's all for the best.

Funny how frost can dance and then flop,
Each pirouette and twirl brings a plop.
The winter sun chuckled, a rascal in bloom,
"Let's leave them to play in this brightening room!"

But hold on to laughter, my dear winter friends,
For the frost will return, round the snowy bends.
In the frosty ballet we always engage,
Every icy laugh is a moment to stage!

Luminous Thaw

The snowman checked his watch, so keen,
Said, "Time's a-wasting, look at my sheen!"
But when the sun poked with a grin,
He melted down, gave in to gin.

His carrot nose rolled down the street,
"Hold onto your hats!" shouted his feet,
With puddles laughing, all around,
A slippery dance, they twirled unbound.

Kids on sleds flew with delight,
Till they splashed in a puddle, what a sight!
"Goodbye, my friend, you were quite spry!"
But alas! A raincloud waved goodbye.

So here's to snowmen, fleeting, bright,
With their floppy hats and funny plight,
Next winter they'll return, no doubt,
But for now, they're all washed out!

Breath of Winter's Passing

The frost choked a giggle, a chilly joke,
A snowflake shouted, "Can I get a poke?"
But each little flake, they started to melt,
Creating tiny puddles, oh what they felt!

Then came the sun with a cheeky grin,
"Let's warm things up, let the fun begin!"
Snowball fights turned to splashy brawls,
As laughter echoed over snowflake falls.

Snowmen played hide and seek, how neat!
"I'm not here!" said one, concealing his feet,
But as they shrank in the sun's warm tease,
They yelled, "Watch out! We're a puddle sneeze!"

With every drip, a tickle and tease,
The end of winter, as fun as a breeze,
A whisper of spring in the melting snow,
Made every drop dance, ready to go!

Snowflurry Reverie

A snowflake landed on a penguin's hat,
"Am I a flake or a cold little brat?"
The penguin chuckled and took to flight,
Leaving the flake in a swirling plight.

Down came the snow, a goofy affair,
Sleds flying high through the frosty air,
But in the chaos and gleeful screeches,
One kid fell backwards, oh how he breaches!

Snowmen turned, curiously wrinkled,
"Why do you kids always behave so sprinkled?"
With carrots your noses, and coal for your eyes,
We're the warmest folks, don't be surprised!

Drifting lightly on a winter's breeze,
The mishaps of snow bring silly tees,
As laughter floats 'neath clouds of white,
This wacky flurry remembered all night!

Frosted Hues

In the garden, frost painted greens,
Turning cabbages into winter's queens,
But they wiggled and jiggled, quite bizarre,
"Who knew we'd be stars at the frosty bazaar?"

The chickens wore scarves, quite out of fashion,
Strutting around with a clucky passion,
"Our feathers need styling, oh what a plight!"
They clucked and they fluffed till the sun said,
"Goodnight!"

Puddles of ice told secrets to snow,
"Watch me slip, watch me slide!" Oh, what a show!
But as they giggled, they fell with a splash,
"Who knew winter would end with such a crash?"

So toast to the frost, the giggles, the fun,
A quirky adventure before spring's run,
In swirling chaos, we dance and we muse,
As laughter blooms bright in the frosted hues!

Gossamer Snowflakes

Fluffy dancers from the skies,
Twirl and giggle, what a surprise!
They land on noses, tickle toes,
Then vanish fast, as laughter flows.

Chasing puffs with frozen breath,
Each one a joke, a wink in death.
They sparkle bright, they ride the breeze,
Like sneaky sprites aimed to tease!

Stray kids tumble, arms out wide,
Hoping for landslides, they collide!
But as they plummet, hearts will race,
Only to melt without a trace.

So grab your mittens, take a shot,
Whirl with joy, give it a thought!
For all that glimmers fades away,
Like giggles gone at end of play.

The Hourglass of Cold

In a snow globe, time slows down,
As chill conquers the sleepy town.
With every tick, the moments freeze,
And icicles giggle in the breeze.

Sipping cocoa, slipping on ice,
Watch your step, it's not so nice!
The chill can tease and make you slip,
Just when you think you've got the grip!

Snowmen grin from yard to yard,
With carrot noses looking charred.
Their smiles say, 'This life is brief!'
While children play and make mischief.

When clocks strike twelve, the trick unfolds,
Frosty dreams are left in molds.
So take a laugh, play in the snow,
Before you know, away they go!

Frosted Whispers

Mysterious murmurs in the chill,
Tell tales of snowflakes, what a thrill!
They giggle softly as they land,
Leaving traces on the frosty sand.

A winded voice, a frosty jest,
Comes dancing by to flurry the rest.
Each flake a whisper, a tiny prank,
As they form mountains by the bank!

Snowball fights erupt with glee,
In this world, we all agree.
Laughter echoes, shy and bright,
As flakes conspire in pure delight.

But when the sun begins to rise,
The laughter fades and snowflakes sigh.
So chase the chill and join the fun,
For jokes are brief, but laughter's spun!

Illusions in Blue

Wandering echoes, ice so bright,
Translucent dreams in morning light.
Children giggle, tumbling down,
Chasing shadows in the town.

Their laughter dances on the stream,
While icy forms begin to beam.
The world is weird, skewed just right,
A game of joy, a frosty fight.

Pop a balloon, watch it float,
As merry jingles sound like a goat!
Snowmen sport their hats with flair,
With eyes that wink, they do not care.

And when the sun steals all the fun,
The jokes dissolve, nowhere to run.
Embrace the mirth while it might last,
For winter laughs fly by so fast!

Quicksilver Winter

Snowflakes dance like little spies,
Whispering secrets, oh how they lie.
A snowman starts to melt away,
Sipping sun like it's a sunny day.

Penguins slip on icy floors,
While polar bears just check their scores.
A snowball fights, a dizzy whirl,
Oops! That punchline made me twirl!

Sleds flying like a rocket ship,
Down the hill, oh what a trip!
Frosty air, a chilly grin,
Giggling loud, let the fun begin!

At dusk, the ice starts to sway,
Saying, "Catch me if you may!"
But you'd fall, oh what a sight,
As winter laughs, "You've lost the fight!"

Memoirs of the Frost

In the grip of winter's flair,
I ponder cheese, the winter fare.
But alas! It's frozen tight,
Even my whiskers feel the bite!

A squirrel mocks the icy breeze,
While birds wear boots upon the trees.
The lake winks with a frosty grin,
"Take a dip? Oh, where to begin?"

Chasing butterflies made of snow,
Caught me slipping on a toe.
A penguin teases with delight,
"Hey there, buddy! Feel the bite!"

As sunsets dip the sky in milk,
I find my hat—a pot of silk.
The frost laughs loud as night awakes,
"Remember, friend, all this can break!"

The Siren's Chill

In Arctic seas, the mermaids sing,
But bring warm tea—oh what a fling!
They swim near shores of frozen glee,
Inviting sailors for a spree.

A ship once sailed with ice cream men,
Who slipped and fell to plank and ken.
"Beware the chill, it's quite the tease!"
The icy song made everyone freeze.

As laughter echoes on the waves,
The frosty mist keeps us all brave.
"Join us, dear, for fun and frolic!"
But the tide mocks, "A bit symbolic!"

The sirens giggle, splash a wave,
"Oops! Consider us quite the knave!"
Yet sailors laugh, with hearts so warm,
As frozen moments become the norm!

Tenuous Tundra

Lost in lands of chilly fun,
Where icicles glisten in the sun.
A snowflake lands upon my nose,
Tickling senses, oh how it glows!

Chasing foxes in the brisk white,
With frosty paws, they dart, take flight.
I trip and tumble, fall unplanned,
Rolling down like the frosty sand.

Snowshoes clatter, laughter roars,
As yetis polish their ice doors.
"Fancy a dance?" they slyly call,
While I get stuck in a snowball!

Layers of warmth say, "Let's retreat!"
But with a wink, I can't admit defeat.
The tundra smiles with icy cheer,
Reminding me, I'm still quite here!

Whispers of the Last Flake

A snowflake giggled, not one to last,
It fluttered and flopped, how long could it cast?
"I'm here for a wink, just a blink in the sky,"
Then plopped in a puddle, it let out a sigh.

The sun gave a chuckle, the clouds rolled their eyes,
As the flake spread its wings, to take one last rise.
"It's warm in the stream, let's have a quick splash!"
But oops, there it goes, in a glorious crash!

Friends gathered 'round, with tales of the freeze,
"Remember that one that danced with the breeze?"
But that flake was gone, just a ripple in time,
It left us its giggles, oh, what a good rhyme!

So here's to the flakes, with their whimsical fate,
They teach us to laugh, and not to just wait!
For life can be silly, it's quick to be shared,
In a blink it will vanish, so let's be prepared!

The Quiet Thaw

Once glimmering frost shone with dazzling pride,
But warmth tiptoed in, oh, what a slick slide!
The grass peeks so green, a joke on the run,
While icicles giggle and melt in the sun.

Puddles now laughing, they dance in the street,
"Who left me so soggy? Life's really a treat!"
The flowers all snicker, their heads up so high,
As the chilly old winter just waves a goodbye.

A snowman named Bob wore a grin and a hat,
His friends made of snow had just sunk like a mat.
"Hey guys, let's do brunch as we slowly dissolve,"
But brunch wasn't happening, just puddles to solve!

So here's to the thaw, with its sneaky warm grace,
It turns icy tales into giggles in space!
For nothing's forever, it's all just a tease,
So chuckle with me, in the warm spring breeze!

Explorations in Crystal

Tiny ice castles in the chill of the night,
Each flake on a journey, oh, what a delight!
Adventure awaits in a shimmer of white,
Where snowmen hold meetings, their laughter so bright.

Take care when you step, for the ice is so sly,
It whispers sweet nothings, then goes with a sigh.
"I'm brave on this surface!" the skater will boast,
But the crack of a fracture will shatter that ghost.

Frosty friends gather for a frosty good time,
Who knew that cold secrets would tickle and rhyme?
As the ice melts away, they'll ink it in ink,
With giggles and polka dots, they'll marinate pink!

So let's find the humor in life's slippery game,
As we glide on the surface, we're never the same.
For laughter's a treasure, like snowflakes in flight,
And our hearts dance along in the soft, glowing light!

A Dance on Thin Ice

Oh, the thrill of the glimmer, but watch how you dance,
For the surface is fickle, it loves to entrance!
With a wiggle and jiggle, you'll slip on surprise,
And go tumbling down with wide-opened eyes!

A snowflake's delight, paired with a frosty twist,
Causing dizzying spins that you never could resist!
They twirl and they swirl, then they clap with great cheer,
When they splat on the ground, and their laughter rings clear!

But oops goes the skater, with arms all akimbo,
As they glide with a splash like a frosty muzzled rainbow!
"Best dance ever!" they yell, from a puddle of glee,
While ducks start to quack, "Is that you, or just me?"

So gather your pals for this zesty cold frolic,
With slips and with spins, it's a giggly cholic!
For life's just a dance on a stage made of ice,
And laughter's the song in this slippery slice!

Changing Patterns on a Frozen Canvas

The sun's a painter with a twist,
It brushes frost and then it missed.
Snowmen dance on shaky feet,
While penguins slide to get a treat.

Frosty art, a fleeting show,
A masterpiece that's doomed to go.
The kids laugh, making snowball fights,
As winter bids its last good nights.

Like swirling dancers on a stage,
They pirouette, then turn the page.
The icy gloss begins to fade,
And puddles form in frosty glade.

Oh slippery fun, it's such a race,
Try not to fall, but what a chase!
Nature's jest is hard to take,
When every step feels like a quake.

A Glimpse of Beauty Before the Melt

A frosty gem on window's pane,
Glistens bright, but not for gain.
A fleeting wink, a soft goodbye,
Like laughing clouds in the sky.

The snowflakes whisper little jokes,
As icy jokers dance with folks.
"Catch me quick!" they seem to cheer,
But they'll soon vanish from here.

Racing kids with faces aglow,
Slip and slide, oh what a show!
But with the sun, sighs fill the air,
"My snowman's gone, but hey, I swear!"

From frosty blooms to drippy streams,
Life's just bursting at the seams.
Laughing as the shadows dwindle,
Nature's giggles now a twinkle.

Fleeting Frost

Frosty coats on bushes cling,
Like coats on cats that don't want spring.
They shimmer bright, make us laugh,
But disappear, like a photo graph.

Snowflakes tumble, a joyful twirl,
As giggling children start to whirl.
Each one unique, then gone with glee,
Like last week's plans—who could foresee?

Slipping here and sliding there,
Winter wonders fill the air.
"Watch out!" they shout with joyful squeals,
As noses giggle and laughter steals.

But as the sunlight starts to grow,
The frosty fun begins to slow.
With splashes, puddles mark their trail,
As winter laughs, "You'll soon set sail!"

Whispering Crystals

Crystals wink from snowy trees,
"Hey there, watch as we freeze!"
With a chuckle, they decide to glow,
But soon they'll have to let it go.

Snotty noses, cheeks all red,
Falling down, it's fun instead!
But those glistening jokes don't last,
Just like the winter's wicked blast.

The giggling frost with teasing flair,
Promised fun in the chilly air.
But as spring peeks, we must relent,
"Goodbye!" they wave—what a funny event!

So let's enjoy this frosty tease,
Before they melt like forgotten cheese.
Winter's laughter, bright and grand,
Will drift away, just like the sand.

Snowfall Serenade

Fluffy flakes dance in the air,
They tickle my nose, I can't help but stare.
A snowman I build with a carrot for a hat,
He wobbles and giggles, now imagine that!

The dog zooms by, chasing shadows of white,
He leaps through the drifts, what a goofy sight!
I slip and I slide on my icy front lawn,
Like a penguin on skates, till the sun greets the dawn.

A snowflake tickles, it settles on my cheek,
I catch it and laugh, nature's mystique!
With frosty high fives, winter's sly play,
It's straight-up confetti, on this snowy day!

As we cheer and we joke, our hands turn to ice,
Hot cocoa awaits, oh, isn't that nice?
With laughter and warmth as we thaw from the freeze,
Winter's a prankster, but one that I seize!

The Iced Ephemeral

Ice cubes jiggle in my drink, it's true,
But they really won't last, like my dignity too.
The fridge hums a tune, so cool and absurd,
While I sip and I grin, oh haven't you heard?

A popsicle fumbles, slips from my hand,
It topsy-turvies onto the soft, hot sand.
A sticky surprise, flavored like dreams,
Melting away like my ambition it seems!

Frosty decorations, flavors that blend,
A snow cone parade, how can this end?
With laughter that bubbles in each chilly bite,
It's a merry-go-round on a frosty delight!

But alas, with the sun, all the magic will fade,
Every bright frozen moment a sweet charade.
So let's dance through the ice while it tickles our toes,
And shake hands with winter before summer shows!

Glimmers of the Unseen

Glittering worlds on the edge of the night,
Each sliver of frost sings a flash of delight.
The garden's a wonderland, a glimmering show,
Where lawn gnomes wear snow hats, just look at them glow!

Mittens on rabbits, a snowdrift parade,
Sleds made of chaos, what plans have we laid?
With giggles and whoops, we race down the hill,
Then tumble in snow, and it's all quite a thrill!

Frosty breath dances with joy in the air,
While icicles shimmer, a winter affair.
The moon plays a prank, casting shadows so long,
Making us laugh with its whimsical song!

So here's to the magic that flits in the freeze,
To moments that sparkle and playful degrees.
In this wondrous ballet of seasons that blend,
Let's toast to the fun, on winter we depend!

Celestial Frost

Stars in the night with a frosty glow,
Whispering secrets only winter can know.
I gaze at Orion, he's frozen in space,
Winking at me with his icy embrace.

Snowflakes flutter like tiny balloons,
They drift through the sky, singing winter tunes.
I tried to catch one, but it giggled and flew,
See, laughter's contagious in the coldest of dew!

Frosted gnomes dance with joy by the moon,
They slide on their bellies, like clowns in a tune.
The crunch of the snow beneath my big feet,
Turns every step into a whimsical beat!

So lift up your hearts like a snowflake in flight,
As laughter and frost wrap us cozy tonight.
With celestial wonders that twinkle and tease,
We'll giggle and shiver, it's sure to appease!

The Brief Embrace of Winter's Touch

Oh, winter's hug lasts not too long,
A fleeting joy, yet feels so strong.
We slip and slide with giggles bright,
As snowballs soar in comical flight.

With every chill, a grin appears,
We laugh away our frosty fears.
The snowman grins, a funny chap,
Till warmth arrives, and he does nap.

A snowflake lands upon my nose,
I sneeze and watch it melt, who knows?
The cold may tease, but let us cheer,
For each brief flicker, winter's here!

In sweaters thick, we bundle tight,
Embracing cold, a frosty sight.
Yet spring will laugh, and take its turn,
As ice melts down, we'll soon discern!

Shimmering Ghosts of Frosted Past

In the morn, the frost does glisten,
Like childhood dreams that still can listen.
We chase the sparkles, skip and run,
While icy trails bring laughter fun.

A snowman wearing dad's old hat,
With twiggy arms and a frozen spat.
His carrot nose, a bit askew,
He winks at me, like he just knew.

Each frosty breath, a cloud of cheer,
As memories swirl, oh so near.
We share our tales of snowy days,
While melting shimmers fade, we praise.

Those ghostly flakes with charms that tease,
All vanish fast, and so do we.
But laughter's scent will linger on,
As winter fades, our joy lives strong!

Shimmering Ghosts of Frosted Past

In the morn, the frost does glisten,
Like childhood dreams that still can listen.
We chase the sparkles, skip and run,
While icy trails bring laughter fun.

A snowman wearing dad's old hat,
With twiggy arms and a frozen spat.
His carrot nose, a bit askew,
He winks at me, like he just knew.

Each frosty breath, a cloud of cheer,
As memories swirl, oh so near.
We share our tales of snowy days,
While melting shimmers fade, we praise.

Those ghostly flakes with charms that tease,
All vanish fast, and so do we.
But laughter's scent will linger on,
As winter fades, our joy lives strong!

The Brief Embrace of Winter's Touch

Oh, winter's hug lasts not too long,
A fleeting joy, yet feels so strong.
We slip and slide with giggles bright,
As snowballs soar in comical flight.

With every chill, a grin appears,
We laugh away our frosty fears.
The snowman grins, a funny chap,
Till warmth arrives, and he does nap.

A snowflake lands upon my nose,
I sneeze and watch it melt, who knows?
The cold may tease, but let us cheer,
For each brief flicker, winter's here!

In sweaters thick, we bundle tight,
Embracing cold, a frosty sight.
Yet spring will laugh, and take its turn,
As ice melts down, we'll soon discern!

Impermanence etchings on a Frozen Lake

The lake, a mirror, shines so bright,
But with each step, it tends to bite.
We skate and slip, a real ballet,
While giggles echo, 'Come what may!'

An ice-cold dip could be in store,
As we chase dreams upon the floor.
But nothing's sure, it starts to crack,
With every glide, we watch our back.

Sketches made by clumsy feet,
Turn to whispers, then retreat.
We dance with ghosts, who laugh and jive,
Before our fleeting fun can thrive.

So let's embrace the chilly dance,
Before the sun steals our last chance.
For every twirl and slip and slide,
Is just a laugh on winter's ride!

Transient Beauty of Snowflakes' Flight

Look up, behold the dancing flakes,
They flitter down like playful snakes.
Each one unique, a wiggly spree,
Until they land and cease to be.

They whisper secrets, soft and light,
Then melt away, oh what a sight!
We catch them on our tongues, with glee,
As they dissolve, come taste with me!

Bouncing on rooftops, swirling round,
A frosty circus, joy unbound.
Yet as they fall, they know too well,
That every giggle holds a spell.

So grab your mittens, let's go play,
With fleeting friends in a white ballet.
For snowflakes share a laugh, it's true,
In their short dance, they shine for you!

Twilight of the Ice

Frosty friends on a winter's night,
Skating sideways, what a sight!
They slip and slide, hilarity reigns,
Snowball fights turn to frozen pains.

The snowmen dance in a clumsy way,
With carrot noses a bit too gay.
Laughter echoes through the chill,
As we tumble down, then up the hill.

Mittens round, not a glove to find,
Chasing snowflakes, oh what a bind!
A snowball hits, right on the head,
We laugh till we're dizzy, then off to bed.

Ice cream dreams in the frosty air,
Sled rides causing quite the scare.
With each slip and slide, we dare to play,
Creating memories in a snowy ballet.

Crystal Embrace

With a crunch, I step on glittery ground,
Watch it shimmer like magic all around.
Snowflakes swirl in a swirling dance,
Who knew winter could cause such a chance?

A snowdrift greets me, I trip and fall,
Spinning like a ballerina, through it all!
The ice that sparkles, so inviting,
Turns my graceful moves to a slapstick sighting.

Hot cocoa spills in my frosty glove,
I sip and laugh, it's what I love.
Icy tresses on the dogs who bark,
Cheeky snow cats leave a hilarious mark.

As I glide, my scarf takes flight,
Hit by a breeze, it's quite the plight.
Giggles erupt as I chase the tail,
Winter's folly, a comical gale.

Glacial Reverie

Beneath the moon, the ice does gleam,
A slippery dream, or so it would seem.
I tried to impress with a pirouette,
But ended up cold, and soaking wet!

Polar bears laughing, they take the stage,
Waltzing through the snow, like old-age sage.
With furry boots, they stomp about,
While I try hard just to not fall out.

A toasty fire, the goal of the game,
But every few steps, it's never the same.
I tumble and roll, in fashion I lack,
Making snow angels in laid-back whack.

Icicles draping from rooftops that tease,
In the game of winter, I fall to my knees.
Laughter echoes, the winter is wild,
Chasing snowflakes like a giddy child.

Shattering Illusions

I thought I'd glide with grace and pride,
But the ice betrayed, I couldn't hide.
A flurry of snow, a slip and slide,
My dignity gone, like a bumpy ride.

The snowball wars have begun anew,
Targets are set, and oh, who drew?
With mittens soggy and noses red,
The winter warlords feel no dread.

A jolly snowman, crooked but bright,
With a silly grin, brings pure delight.
I beg for mercy, it's all in jest,
Though the chill brings forth a funny test.

Shoveling snow? A backbreaking feat,
With every scoff, my boots retreat.
Yet here I stand, laughter in tow,
As winter plays tricks in a frosty show.